Let's Learn About…

LADYBUGS

By: Breanne Sartori

Introduction

Ladybugs are so pretty! Their red and black shells are quite easy to spot in the garden as they crawl along green bushes. You might think that because they are called "lady" bugs that they are very peaceful. In fact, they're ferocious predators! There's no doubt about it, these bugs are very surprising.

What are Ladybugs

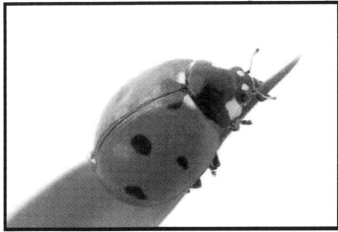

Did you know that ladybugs aren't actually bugs? It's true – they're beetles! In Europe they are often called lady beetles. Strangely, in the UK they call them ladybird beetles!

What Ladybugs Look Like

You're probably familiar with what ladybugs look like. They are usually red with black spots. This can be different for different species though. They have six small legs and they have wings too! Their heads are very small and they have tiny antennae.

Colours and Spots

Ladybugs aren't all red. While it's the most common, ladybugs can be brown, yellow, orange, black and even pink! Not all ladybugs have spots - some have stripes! Not only that, their spots fade as they get older!

Wings

Yes, ladybugs do have wings! You just probably can't see them. This is because when they're not using them, they keep them hidden under their shell. Their shell actually opens up to allow the bugs to use their wings.

Antennae

It's hard to see ladybug antennae because they're so tiny! They sit on the head of the ladybug next to their mouth, not sticking up like most insects. Their antennae are what they use to smell, taste and feel.

Eyes

Ladybugs have two tiny eyes on either side of their head. They aren't very useful though! They can only tell the difference between dark and light, and they can't see colours at all! They rely very heavily on their antennae.

Feet

Can you smell with your feet? You might think it's a funny question, but ladybugs can! Their feet look like little hooks on the ends of their legs. They're very good at clinging onto things, which makes them good climbers!

Where Ladybugs Live

Ladybugs are found all over the world! It is only in the far north and Antarctica that they don't live. They're found in meadows, woods, gardens and farms. Anywhere that it's not too cold and there are lots of plants, you are likely to find them!

Hibernation

A lot of species of ladybug hibernate! As soon as summer ends they get together in big groups and bundle up together. Some people think they do this because they are more likely to survive the winter if they are all together. They release pheromones which are chemicals other ladybugs can smell so that they join each other.

Flying

Ladybugs aren't the best fliers. They can look a little clumsy! This is because their wings aren't free to flap about much. Their shell can get in the way of their wings and they can also have trouble with the wings because they spend so much time folded up and hidden away.

What Ladybugs Eat

Ladybugs are classified as carnivores because they only eat other insects. Their main source of food are aphids, which are little bugs that drink sap from plants. Ladybugs will also eat other small insects, but the average ladybug will eat more than 5,000 aphids each year!

Hunting

Ladybugs eyes are very bad, so they rely heavily on their sense of smell to find food. Their antennae and their feet are both used to pick up the scent of their prey. Ladybugs will walk up and down the stems of a plant to sniff out an aphid.

Farmers Friends

Farmers love having ladybugs in the garden! This is because aphids are a pest! They damage the plants that they feed on. Ladybugs will lay their eggs in aphid nests, wiping them all out. Some farmers choose to put ladybugs in their crops instead of using chemicals!

Cannibalism

If you don't think ladybugs are vicious in the bug world already, you will now. When they are born they will eat each other! This is because when they hatch they are very hungry and need to start eating immediately. Some of the others are unlucky enough to be in the way.

Baby Ladybugs

Baby ladybugs have two stages – larvae and pupa stage. When the ladybug is still a larvae, it doesn't look anything like a ladybug! It's long and dark grey in colour. The pupa is the next stage where it looks sort of like a yellow worm. This is the stage where metamorphosis takes place, which is when they develop into an adult!

Breeding

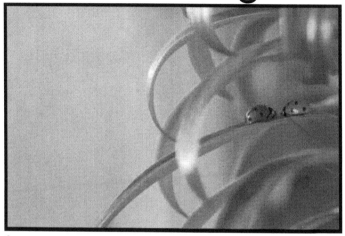

Ladybugs attract each other using pheromones, which are chemicals that other ladybugs can smell. The female can store the sperm from the male for months before deciding to use it to fertilise her eggs. She will then lay her eggs on leaves in bunches, which kind of look like yellow rice grains!

The Life of a Lady Bug

Ladybugs go through three stages of life –
the larvae, pupa and then the adult. It takes
a few weeks for a ladybug to develop into
an adult. Once grown, they will only live for
2 years. When the adult first breaks out of
the pupa, it's actually soft and pink! It takes
a few hours before the shell becomes hard
and gets darker.

Predators

Even though they are great predators, ladybugs are still prey to a lot of other animals. Birds, lizards, frogs, rodents and other insects will all eat ladybugs when given the opportunity. Some only target their eggs, larvae or pupa though.

Protecting Themselves

Ladybugs aren't completely defenceless, but they don't have any weapons. To protect themselves they rely on their predators thinking that they will taste gross! This is the reason for the brightly coloured shell. They also play dead and squeeze out yellow goo from their legs, which looks gross!

Other Dangers

Like a lot of other animals, ladybugs face danger from humans. Not only do we accidentally kill a lot of them, we destroy their environment. Because ladybugs are very sensitive to the temperature, climate change is very dangerous for them. They are considered endangered, which means they might become extinct.

30726880R00015

Made in the USA
Middletown, DE
04 April 2016